the skinny on™

15 POINTS FOR IMPROVING WILLPOWER AND SELF-DISCIPLINE

1. Be sure you are totally committed.

2. Prepare yourself for a difficult journey.

3. Prepare for your challenge by reducing the instances in which you will need to exert willpower.

4. Identify your goal and the process to get there in as concrete, specific, and finite terms as possible.

5. Divide your challenge into small, manageable pieces.

6. Maintain vigilance over your thoughts.

7. Control your dominant thoughts.

8. Frame your challenges in a pleasurable, not painful, manner.

9. Pick your spots.

10. Force yourself to visualize the end of a succession of "either/or" choices.

www.theskinnyon.com

Pssst ... get
the skinny on™
life's most
important lessons

www.theskinnyon.com

The Easiest Learning There Is!!

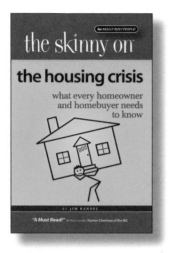

11. You already have more willpower than you realize.

12. The more you use your willpower, the more confidence and strength you have for new challenges.

13. Turn positive activity into habits.

14. Self-discipline is not self-deprivation.

15. Strong willpower can take you to new heights in life.

"Willpower isn't something that gets handed out to some and not to others, ... it's a skill you can develop through understanding and practice."

Gillian Riley

The Skinny on Willpower

the skinny on™
willpower

how to develop self-discipline

Jim Randel

ISBN: 978-0-9818935-3-2
Illustration: Malinda Nass ☺

For information address RAND Publishing, 265 Post Road West,
Westport, CT, 06880 or call (203) 226-8727.

The Skinny On™ books are available for special promotions and premiums.
For details contact: Donna Hardy, call (203) 222-6295 or visit our website:
www.theskinnyon.com

Printed in the United States of America

"The one quality which sets one apart from another – the key which lifts one to every aspiration while others are caught up in the mire of mediocrity – is not talent, formal education, nor intellectual brightness; it is self-discipline. With self-discipline, all things are possible. Without it, even the simplest goal can seem like the impossible dream."

Teddy Roosevelt
26th President of the United States

the skinny on™

Welcome to a new series of publications entitled **The Skinny On**™, a progression of drawings, dialogue and text intended to convey information in a concise fashion.

In our time-starved and information-overloaded culture, most of us have far too little time to read and absorb major important writings and research on important topics. So, our understanding tends to float on the surface – without the benefit of the thinking of the writers and teachers who have spent years studying these topics.

Our series is intended to address this situation. Our team of readers and researchers has done a ton of homework in preparing our books for you. We have read just about everything respected author on a particular topic and distilled what we learned into this "skinny" book for your benefit.

You might think of our book as concentrated learning. By spending one or two hours reading our book, we maintain that you get the benefit of the hundreds of hours you would spend reading all the works on a particular subject.

Our goal is to do the reading for you, cull out what is important, distill the key points and present them in a book that we hope is both instructive and entertaining.

Although minimalist in design, we do take our message very seriously. Please do not confuse format with content. The time you invest reading this book will be paid back to you many, many times over.

FOREWORD

For many years, I have studied the process of achievement. I have read everything I could find on the subject; I have pestered highly successful friends and acquaintances as to their own path to success; and I have experimented with my own life. Here is what I have concluded:

99% of those individuals who achieve their goals do so not because they are especially talented, intelligent, good-looking or even lucky, but rather because they find the courage and guts to act in pursuit of their dreams and persist against setbacks.

One of the reasons I have written *The Skinny on Willpower* is because I worry that people with dreams have been distracted by authors sending people this message:

"The Universe is rooting for you. If you just ask, put your belief in the Universe and be patient, your wishes will come true."

I do not believe that statement. I have seen people get lucky (and I say "good for them"), but 99% of the people I have seen achieve their dreams have done so with hard work, determination, persistence and guts. In other words, if you want good things to happen in your life, you need to get off the couch and make them happen.

Whether your goal is to lose weight, make a million dollars, write a best-seller, or become a movie star, you must be prepared to pay the price. Those people who accomplish their dreams are usually distinguished by the strength of their will.

You are about to read a book that will help bring you closer to your dreams and goals by giving you insight into the subject of willpower. As Teddy Roosevelt said: "With self-discipline, all things are possible."

INTRODUCTION

Willpower – the strength to act, or forbear from acting in the pursuit of a goal – is a critical determinant to success.

With any goal, there are times when action is needed ("I should go to the gym") and times when forbearance is needed ("I should not have dessert"). What happens between one's thought and one's response is the result of one's willpower, or lack thereof.

Freud described the mind as "an arena, a sort of tumbling ground, for the struggle of antagonistic impulses," and that's the reason people need willpower. At times, we all find it hard to take appropriate action in the face of competing pressures, impulses or temptations.

In doing our homework for this book, we read or listened to everything we could find on the subjects of willpower and self-discipline – books, articles and CDs. We spoke with professors and researchers. We spent hours online looking for insight. We interviewed highly successful people – movie and TV celebrities, professional and Olympic athletes, well-known politicians, CEOs of Fortune 500 companies and really rich entrepreneurs. Our conclusions are the results of both personal experience and all that we learned from others.

Our goal is to teach you all that we have learned. We hope that by doing so, we will give you ideas for adapting your behavior in the development of the willpower you may need to achieve your personal goals.

So get comfortable. Give us about an hour to read about Billy and Beth's struggles with the willpower they need to accomplish their goals. We hope that at the end of your read, you will have a better sense of the topic and will thereby be a little closer to the achievement of your own aspirations.

"OK, Billy, I'm with you all the way. Here, let me rub your belly for good luck before it disappears!"

8

BUT BETH HAS DOUBTS ABOUT BILLY STICKING TO A DIET. SHE'S SEEN HIM START AND STOP BEFORE.

I'll be surprised if he can give up marshmallows.

9

IS BILLY HOOKED ON MARSHMALLOWS?

Well, not just marshmallows – Billy loves all sweets.

We mentioned marshmallows as a segue to telling you about one of the most famous studies ever undertaken on the subject of willpower.

In the early 1960's a Stanford psychologist, Dr. Walter Mischel, picked an unlikely group to test his theories: **four-year-olds**!

Here's the setup:

Thirty or so four-year-olds are in a classroom. The teacher stands in the front of the room holding a tray filled with marshmallows. Here is what the teacher says:

"Each of you can have a marshmallow right now. But I have to leave for a little while, and if you wait until I return, then you can have *two* marshmallows."

This test, of course, would try the soul of any four-year-old, and about a third of the children took the one marshmallow right away.

Others decided to try and wait. Many of those who did found ways to distract themselves.

Some covered their eyes ... some talked or sang to themselves ... some played with their hands and feet ... some tried to go to sleep.

MARSHMALLOW MADNESS

After about 15 minutes (which I am sure seemed like an eternity to the children), the teacher returned and those who had not taken a marshmallow were given two.

Now here is the interesting part:

Fourteen years later, as this same group of thirty was graduating high school, they were surveyed again.

Dr. Mischel compared the students on a variety of criteria including performance in schoolwork, social skills and popularity. What he found is that the four-year-olds who were able to exercise willpower and wait for the two marshmallows generally had greater success in all aspects of their high school years.

Certainly this test was just a rough measure of the willpower-achievement connection, and those of you reading this book who may have less-than-patient four-year-olds (is there truly such a thing as a patient four-year-old?), no worries:

Psychologists agree that different children acquire willpower at different times in their young lives. And that adults, too, can improve their willpower and self-discipline at any age.

BETH IS NOT SURE ABOUT BILLY'S WILLPOWER.

"Billy, you just ate an entire bag of marshmallows."

"I did???"

13

BILLY, TOO, HAS CONCERNS ABOUT HIS ABILITY TO LOSE WEIGHT.

However, unlike his previous tries, this time he has taken two important steps in the right direction:

1. He was **specific** as to the exact amount of weight he wanted to lose.

2. He made a **commitment** to (a contract with) himself.

14

Billy expressing steely resolve.

1. THE IMPORTANCE OF BEING SPECIFIC

Numerous studies have shown that when people define their goal in exact terms, they are much more likely to be successful.

As an example, most dieters who define their goal in discrete terms ("I will lose **ten pounds**") perform better than those whose goal is vague ("I will slim down.")

In an excellent textbook on the study of human behavior, Professor Johnmarshall Reeve of the University of Iowa gives several illustrations of how we perform more successfully when we know **exactly what we need to do**.

Understanding Motivation and Emotion,
Reeve (Wiley, 2008)

Professor Reeve teaches us that in all endeavors, those who have a definite target, i.e., a specific goal, outperform those who do not.

In one study of elementary school students (why are researchers always picking on kids?), students were divided into two groups of equal athletic ability. One group of students set a specific goal as to the number of sit-ups they would do; the other did not. After two minutes, the goal-setting students finished significantly more sit-ups than did the no-goal students.

The same result was found in many other studies. Loggers with specific goals outperformed others. So did word processors and truck drivers.

Professor Reeve: "Telling a performer 'do your best' sounds like goal-setting, but it is actually only an ambiguous statement that does not make clear precisely what the person is to do.... Translating a vague goal into a specific goal typically involves restating the goal in numerical terms. **Goal specificity is important because specific goals reduce ambiguity in thought and variability in performance.**"

(Emphasis Added)

2. THE IMPORTANCE OF MAKING A COMMITMENT TO YOURSELF

One way of looking at willpower is that it is the execution of a contract a goal-setter makes with himself.

"I am finally going to _____" (fill in the blank with one of your goals) are words that many of us have said to ourselves.

Those who treat those words as an **inviolate contract** that cannot be broken often find the willpower and resolve they need to accomplish their goal.

"Discipline is a contract with yourself. A contract you must adhere to, regardless of the circumstances. You are the cop; break the rules and you fail."

Discipline, Harris Kern (1st Books, 2001).

One of the great stories in achievement lore is that of the actor, Jim Carrey.

Carrey came to Los Angeles without a penny to his name, determined to make it in show business. So, he made a contract with himself:

He actually wrote a check to himself for $10,000,000, which he postdated five years from the date he wrote it.

And 3 or 4 years later, after the success of *Ace Ventura: Pet Detective* and other big movies, Carrey was, in fact, able to cash the check he had written to himself.

Certainly a big part of Jim Carrey's path to success was willpower.

When he arrived in Hollywood from his home in Canada, there were no producers waiting for him with open arms. He had to scratch and claw his way into auditions and hold onto his dreams even when all signs were that he was going nowhere.

But by writing himself a check, Carrey created a positive affirmation that he was going to succeed: he made a contract with himself (the postdated check) and he was very specific as to what his goal was ($10,000,000).

Here are Carrey's words:

"When I wasn't doing anything in this town (Hollywood), I'd go up every night, sit on Mulholland Drive, look out to the city, stretch out my arms, and say:

'Everybody wants to work with me.'

I'd just repeat these things over and over, literally convincing myself that I had a couple of movies lined up. I'd drive down the hill, ready to take the world on, going:

'Movie offers are out there for me,
I just don't hear them yet.' "

CARREY'S STORY IS AN ILLUSTRATION OF:

The Power of Positive Thinking

Perhaps the best-known book on the subject of goal attainment is *The Power of Positive Thinking* (Fawcett, 1952), written by Dr. Norman Vincent Peale.

Peale believed that we all have the inner strength to achieve our goals and dreams. The key is to activate this strength with a wholehearted approach to our goal:

"People are defeated in life not because of lack of ability, but for lack of wholeheartedness.... Give every bit of yourself. Hold nothing back. Life cannot deny itself to the person who gives life his all."

Peale believed that willpower and resolve, an unwillingness to give in to setbacks, were critical to success:

"Altogether too many people are defeated by the everyday problems of life.... (But) by learning how to cast (negative thoughts) from the mind, by refusing to become mentally subservient to them, and by channeling spiritual power through your thoughts, you can rise above obstacles which ordinarily might defeat you."

Dr. Norman Vincent Peale

As you see, Dr. Peale, and many authors since, speak to the need for a positive mental attitude in order to achieve one's goals.

And, of course, I agree.

But, to me, that begs the question:

HOW DOES ONE DEVELOP A POSITIVE MENTAL ATTITUDE?

Certainly, some people are fortunate and they are born with an optimistic, can-do attitude. However, for most of us, a positive mental attitude is something we need to acquire over time.

As we will discuss in the pages that follow, there are identifiable steps you can take to help you develop the confidence and optimism you need to accomplish your goals.

Here are three suggestions for developing a positive mindset; we will be discussing each in more detail later:

1. **Break up a challenge** into small, manageable pieces. With the achievement of each part, your confidence grows, allowing you to master challenges of increasing difficulty.

2. Teach yourself to **eject negativism from your mind**. The great martial artist, Bruce Lee, would actually write down negative thoughts on a piece of paper and set the paper on fire.

3. **Find strength** in the fact that you are the product of thousands of years of evolution and, as a survivor, are already equipped with the tools you need to accomplish your goals – you just need to activate them.

Back to Billy and Beth

THAT EVENING

"Billy, you've inspired me ... I've made a New Year's resolution too."

"Great, Beth. What is it?"

"Well, you know I've always dreamed of opening my own clothing store. I'm finally going to do it!"

"That's wonderful, Beth.
I'm sure you will be a
huge success."

29

30

It's cute that Billy and Beth are so supportive of each other's New Year's resolutions. They can turn to each other if and when their resolve weakens.

On the other hand, some writers suggest keeping our resolutions to ourselves. Except for very dear friends, there will always be naysayers whose comments may diminish your willpower.

Can you hear the laughter of Jim Carrey's buddies if, when he arrived in Hollywood, he shared with them the existence of the $10,000,000 check he wrote to himself?

Perhaps now is the time to make one other point about willpower and achievement:

NO ONE SIZE FITS ALL!!

What's best for one person may not be best for another.

Billy and Beth chose to share their resolutions with each other and gained strength from the other's support.

I tend to keep my goals to myself.

HOW ABOUT YOU?

If you like to keep goals to your-self, write your goal here:

_____

Why?

Because then you won't give this book to anyone, and I'll sell more books.

Enough great humor for now.

Billy and Beth are having dinner at Billy's mother's house.

Let's check in.

"Gee, Mom, that was a great dinner."

"Oh, we're not done yet. I've baked your favorite chocolate cake for dessert."

Is Billy's mom right?

"Moderation in all things."

Well, many willpower thinkers would argue the reverse: that there are times when one needs to go "cold turkey" – an all-or-nothing approach – for example, no desserts at all until one's weight goal is reached.

The problem with moderation is that it requires **ad hoc decisions**, which in turn require energy.

For example, if every time Billy is tempted to eat sweets, he has to make a decision whether to indulge or not, **he will expend energy in the process of deliberation** – energy that he needs to preserve for acts of willpower.

And, as we will discuss again and again in this book, **the proper application of energy** is a BIG DEAL when it comes to having self-discipline when you need it.

So far today, I've had about 1,500 calories ... or is it 2,000? This cake is 300 calories. I could go for a run tomorrow. That will burn 400 calories.

HERE ARE THREE EXPERTS WHO SPEAK TO THE ALL-OR-NOTHING APPROACH:

1. Jack Canfield

Canfield is the highly successful author of the *Chicken Soup* series. Canfield has also written a comprehensive book on the subject of success, *The Success Principles: How to Get from Where You Are to Where You Want to Be* (Harper Collins, 2005).

In this book, Canfield speaks to his "No Exceptions Rule."

"Successful people adhere to the 'no exceptions rule' when it comes to their daily disciplines. Once you make a 100% commitment to something, there are no exceptions. It's a done deal. Nonnegotiable. Case closed!

"(Once a decision has been made), I don't have to wrestle with that decision every day. It's already been made. The die has been cast. All the bridges are burned. It makes life easier and simpler and keeps me on focus. It frees up tons of energy that would otherwise be spent internally debating the topic over and over and over … and all the energy I expend on internal conflict is unavailable to use for creating outer achievement."

2. Dr. William James

And then there is perhaps our greatest American psychologist, William James.

James was a Harvard-trained MD who completed his 2,900-page masterpiece, *The Principles of Psychology*, in 1890.

James' view, as paraphrased by his biographer, Robert Richardson, was that when confronted with the need to act (or forbear from negative action), the less deliberation, the better.

"The more we struggle and debate, the more we reconsider and delay, the less likely we are to act (appropriately). Don't wait until you feel better to go to the gym; go to the gym and you will feel better."

William James (Houghton Mifflin, 2007)

AUTHOR'S NOTE

As you know, we at **The Skinny On**™ believe that "less is more" – that an author should endeavor to use as few words as possible to convey his or her thoughts. That requires editing and more editing – showing respect for a reader's time and attention.

And William James made the same point upon delivering his 2,900-page treatise on psychology to his publisher:

"Had I ten years more, I could rewrite it in 500 (pages), but as it stands it is … a loathsome, distended, tumefied, bloated, dropsical mass…."

To be contrasted with Canfield and James, here is an expert who does not believe in the all-or-nothing approach:

3. Dr. Howard Rankin

Rankin is a psychologist who studied self-control in England working at the University of London's Addiction Research Unit. His studies taught him that **willpower should be developed incrementally**.

Rankin does not believe in the all-or-nothing approach because he feels that "deprivation is the mother of failure;" in other words, if we are too strict with ourselves, we are most likely going to weaken.

Rankin's approach to self-control is what he calls **graded exposure**, essentially the process of building willpower in small, progressive steps.

For example, he would suggest that a person like Billy, whose willpower is weakened by sweets, do the following:

1. Stand in front of a candy store, look in the window, but do not go in.
2. A few days later, actually walk into the candy store and then immediately walk out.
3. A few days later, go into the candy store and stay for ten minutes, but do not buy anything.
4. A few days later, go into the candy store and buy just one small piece of candy.

The point is that with each step, one develops the ability to resist temptation when and as he or she wants to.

"As your confidence develops and you learn what it feels like to exercise self-control, more difficult situations can be confronted."

THERE IS NO RIGHT ANSWER TO THE "ALL-OR-NOTHING" VERSUS "ALL THINGS IN MODERATION" DEBATE.

EVERYONE NEEDS TO DO WHAT WORKS BEST FOR HIM OR HER.

For me, all-or-nothing works best because I find that I am more likely to stick with a goal if I am inflexible with myself. For example, if I commit to go for a run three times a week, I find that if I set in advance the days I will run, no matter what else is happening (including the weather), then I will run on those days.

My wife, on the other hand, thinks that I am wacky. If she sets a goal that is inflexible, she feels that she has put herself into a box that is uncomfortable right from the start. As a result, she finds that she looks for every opportunity to leave the box – and therefore, an all-or-nothing approach does not work for her.

My wife likes to tell the story of a time I went on a diet and refused her offer of one M & M candy. I told her that if I ate one, I might then eat two and eventually the whole bag. This event caused my wife (able to stop after one M & M) to wonder about me.

Let's check back with Billy and Beth.

The last time we saw Billy he was trying to decide whether to eat a piece of his mom's chocolate cake.

OUCH!

P.S. "Desserts" spelled backwards is: "stressed."

THE NEXT DAY BILLY ATTENDS A YOGA CLASS

"Nice downward dog, Billy, but you seem a little distracted today."

"I'm on a diet, but I can't seem to stick to it."

Made-up saying or not, Billy's yoga instructor has asked Billy an important question.

Does he *really* want to lose weight?

Or was his commitment to lose weight just a wishful thought on the biggest day of the year for hoped-for change: New Year's Day? In fact, maybe Billy in his heart of hearts is OK with his extra poundage.

Here is the point: before you undertake any challenge, be sure that you really, really want what you set out for.

One of the most important lessons I have learned in researching willpower is that its availability to you is directly proportional to the intensity you have for your objective.

In fact, one might argue that the subject of self-discipline is really a measure of how one answers the question:

"How Badly Do You Want It?"

As Professor Reeve has written, people whose motivation is internally activated by a deeply-felt personal belief are much more likely to achieve their objective than those people who are driven by external reward (e.g. money).

"People experience optimal function and positive well-being when they pursue goals that reflect intrinsic motivation … those who pursue intrinsic motivation in life show greater self-actualization and subjective vitality…."

Human Motivation and Emotion (Wiley, 2008)

"Success with willpower simply depends upon what you choose to value."

Willpower, **Gillian Riley (Vermillion, 2003)**

58

Gillian Riley, in her book, *Willpower*, relates the story of an obese woman who after struggling unsuccessfully with her weight for twenty years, finally lost 70 pounds in a matter of months. Her motivation? She discovered that her son needed a kidney-transplant and whereas she was an acceptable donor, the doctors would not operate on her until she lost weight.

"I found the willpower I never knew I had."

59

In many respects willpower boils down to:

(1) Consciousness – maintaining an awareness of your actions and inactions.

(2) Taking ownership of your choices – acknowledging that your action (or inactions) are within your control.

(3) Making the right choices – so much easier to do when you are driven by deeply-seated values.

Once you identify your goal and assess its value to you, the challenge of course is to resist negative pressures and take appropriate actions day in and day out.

"It wasn't a coincidence that I started the story of Billy and Beth on January 1, as that is the one day of the year when so many people make resolutions and set goals. The problem is that most people do not sustain their commitment. What seems so achievable on January 1 often falls by the wayside by January 10."

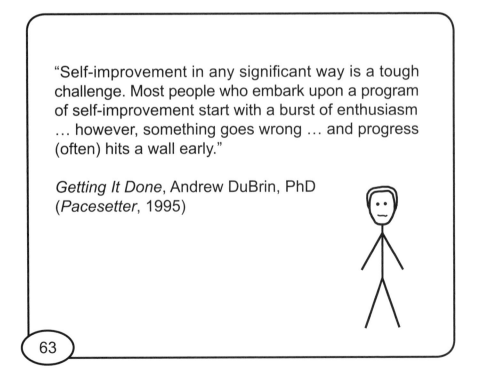

"Self-improvement in any significant way is a tough challenge. Most people who embark upon a program of self-improvement start with a burst of enthusiasm … however, something goes wrong … and progress (often) hits a wall early."

Getting It Done, Andrew DuBrin, PhD (*Pacesetter*, 1995)

DOES IT SURPRISE YOU THAT MORE PEOPLE JOIN HEALTH CLUBS IN JANUARY THAN IN ANY OTHER MONTH?

But by March, most new members have quit.

If you don't believe me, see the report below that concludes (after 28 pages of mathematical analysis) that every New Year's Day many people overestimate their willpower:

> "Contractual choice. At time 0, consumers who sign a contract (T', L', p') expect to attain the net benefit
>
> $$\beta\delta\left[-L + \frac{1-\delta^{T'}}{1-\delta}\int_{-\infty}^{\beta\delta-p'}(\delta b - p' - c)\,dG(c)\right]$$
>
> Our results are difficult to reconcile with the standard assumptions of time-consistent preferences and rational expectations. **A model … with overconfidence about self-control explains the findings**."
>
> *Overestimating Self-Control: Evidence from the Health Club Industry*, Della Vigna and Malmendier

"Geez, who thinks up these studies? They could've just asked me!"

The challenge is not how to burst out of the gate ... whether on January 1 or any other day of the year ... the challenge is HOW TO SUSTAIN the willpower you will need to achieve your goal!

SUSTAIN comes from the Latin *sustinere*, which means TO HOLD UP.

So, the question really is:

When you make a contract with yourself, can you HOLD UP your end of the bargain?

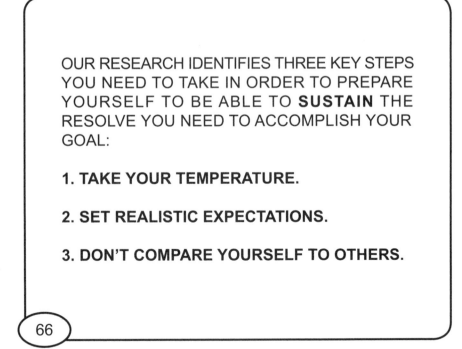

OUR RESEARCH IDENTIFIES THREE KEY STEPS YOU NEED TO TAKE IN ORDER TO PREPARE YOURSELF TO BE ABLE TO **SUSTAIN** THE RESOLVE YOU NEED TO ACCOMPLISH YOUR GOAL:

1. TAKE YOUR TEMPERATURE.

2. SET REALISTIC EXPECTATIONS.

3. DON'T COMPARE YOURSELF TO OTHERS.

1. TAKE YOUR TEMPERATURE

No, not that kind of temperature. What we mean is, ask yourself (as Billy's yoga teach asked him) how badly you want to achieve your goal. One of the most famous self-improvement authors (Napoleon Hill) speaks to the need for "a desire of white-hot intensity." In other words, do you really, really want to achieve your goal? The good news is that if you do, you can almost stop reading.

You know the expression "Where there's a will, there's a way"? Well, many achievement authors would say the same thing a little differently:

"Where there's a will, there's willpower."

In other words, if you want something badly enough, your internal programming (for survival) will kick in and help you find the self-discipline you need along the path to your goal.

But don't kid yourself. If your temperature is not high enough – if you do not want something badly enough – why bother? Your willpower will fade when the going gets tough – and whenever you seek something of value, the going will always get tough.

2. SET REALISTIC EXPECTATIONS

One of the reasons so many people fall by the way-side – in other words, lose the willpower they need when the going gets tough – is that they have not set their expectations properly.

Here is something to remember for the rest of your life:

Nothing good comes easy.

Before you undertake the passage from where you are to where you want to be, tell yourself over and over that **there will be tough times**. Visualize the difficulties if you want to. Ask yourself whether you are ready for the journey.

If you set your expectations correctly – expecting difficulties – your willpower will not wane when the inevitable difficulties appear.

One of my favorite quotes comes from *The Road Less Traveled* (Bantam, 1980), written by Dr. Scott Peck:

"Life is difficult.

"This is a great truth, one of the greatest truths. It is a great truth because once we see this truth, we transcend it. Once we truly know that life is difficult – once we truly understand and accept it – **then life is no longer difficult**."

Dr. Scott Peck

3. DON'T COMPARE YOURSELF TO OTHERS

I find that one reason people lose the will to achieve their goals is that they don't understand that achievement is **tough for everyone**.

They look around them, perhaps at people who seem to get what they want so easily, and conclude that achievers are somehow different. This then causes them to give up, to lose their willpower when confronted with difficulty.

But here is the truth: **every single person** who achieves something of value struggles and at times thinks about quitting. The succeeder is most often simply the person who won't quit.

In doing my research for this book, I spoke with lots of celebrity types – Olympic athletes, famous TV personalities, CEOs of some of our largest corporations, and well-known political figures. They all struggled to achieve their goals.

Just recently one of my neighbors passed away. His name was Paul Newman, and I really admired him – he was not only a great actor, he was successful at whatever he did. I used to assume that everything just came easily to him; that would frustrate me because I would think that my own challenges were harder than his.

Just before he passed away, Paul Newman had this to say:

"Nothing in life ever came easy to me."

Back to Billy

As it happens, he is just now measuring the intensity of his commitment to losing weight.

My yoga instructor is right ... I need to be sure my heart is 100% into dieting.

WHILE BILLY AND BETH ARE SLEEPING, LET'S RECAP BY CONSIDERING THESE QUESTIONS:

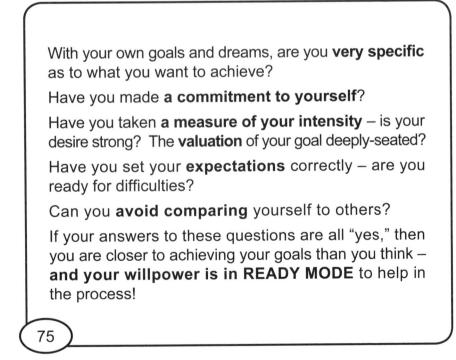

With your own goals and dreams, are you **very specific** as to what you want to achieve?

Have you made **a commitment to yourself**?

Have you taken **a measure of your intensity** – is your desire strong? The **valuation** of your goal deeply-seated?

Have you set your **expectations** correctly – are you ready for difficulties?

Can you **avoid comparing** yourself to others?

If your answers to these questions are all "yes," then you are closer to achieving your goals than you think – **and your willpower is in READY MODE** to help in the process!

The next morning

"Wait, Beth –
stop! That's my
Fruity Hoops
cereal. Fruit is
good for me."

"Out of the way, silly
man! Fruity Hoops
are sweetened
with sugar."

This is going to be really hard!!!

82

Of course, Beth is right about Fruity Hoops … but this book is not about cereals.

What it is about is willpower, and the point I want to make here is that **marketers are brilliant** at subverting your resolve.

Whatever they want to sell you, marketers are good at getting into your head and trying to break down your self-discipline.

Whether their goal is to get you to buy their cereals, smoke their cigarettes, or use their credit cards (beyond a reasonable limit), marketers are good at playing with your will.

These people are not on your side. Please watch for our upcoming book, ***The Skinny on Credit Cards***, and in the meantime, be wary of slick marketing.

83

BETH, TOO, HAS BEEN WORKING ON HER RESOLUTION – TO OPEN A CLOTHING STORE.

SHE HAS BEEN TO A BANK FOR A LOAN.

BUT THEY WANT TO SEE A BUSINESS PLAN.

"Good morning, Beth. You were up early. What are you doing?"

"I'm trying to write a business plan."

"Beth, so many people have great ideas but then never act on them. The problem is inertia."

WHAT IS INERTIA?

Inertia is a law of physics. Actually, inertia is two laws, the first of which says that:

#1: A property of matter **remains at rest** unless acted upon by an external force.

"Inertia is a very powerful force that keeps people from moving forward toward their goals and dreams.

Often, the biggest challenge is just the first step."

Willpower is the effort needed to **get going** in a forward motion.

Sometimes it is finding the strength to get out of bed on a cold morning when lying under the covers is so much more appealing. Sometimes it is finding the resolve to type the first sentence of a term paper, a book … or a business plan. Sometimes it is that first visit to a gym when you haven't been in a long time.

Inertia is defeated when you steel yourself, focus all your energy, push back on any competing pressures and **move forward**.

And the second part of inertia says that:

#2: A property of matter **remains in motion** unless acted upon by an external force.

Inertia can be a great friend once a person marshals the willpower to move forward in the pursuit of a goal or dream.

That is because the law of inertia also says that once a body is in motion, it will continue to stay in motion unless stopped by an outside force.

So, once you start moving in the right direction, nature will be working for you. The wind starts to blow at your back, carrying you forward.

"This is a very important point and I want to elaborate."

Once inertia is working in your favor, activities that once required self-discipline start to become habits. When activities become habits, less and less self-discipline is necessary to accomplish them.

By way of example, when you were a youngster, your parents may have had to remind you to brush your teeth. Then this activity became a habit.

Now brushing your teeth does not require willpower. You are on "automatic pilot."

HERE ARE THREE BOOKS THAT AMPLIFY THE POINT:

1. In *The Creative Habit* (Simon & Schuster, 2006) choreographer Twyla Tharp describes how important habits are to her success:

   "My morning workout ritual is the most basic form of self-reliance; rituals … arm us with confidence and self-reliance."

2. In *The Power of Full Engagement* (Free Press, 2003) authors Jim Loehr and Tony Schwartz make the point that habits actually replace the need for self-discipline:

   "We can offset our limited will and discipline by building rituals that become automatic.…"

3. In *The Seven Habits of Highly Effective People* (Simon & Schuster, 1989) Stephen Covey proclaims the power of habit:

   "Because they are consistent, often unconscious patterns, they constantly, daily, express our character and produce our effectiveness.…"

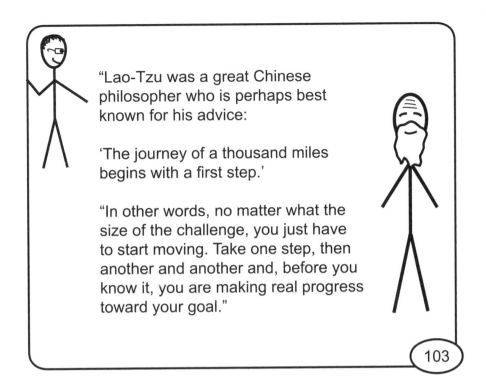

"Lao-Tzu was a great Chinese philosopher who is perhaps best known for his advice:

'The journey of a thousand miles begins with a first step.'

"In other words, no matter what the size of the challenge, you just have to start moving. Take one step, then another and another and, before you know it, you are making real progress toward your goal."

103

"I don't get this guy, Beth."

"Shh ... I'm typing."

"Bye, now."

104

BIG
MISTAKE,
BILLY.

Billy has made the classic mistake that so many make when in pursuit of a goal. He binged, looking for results too quickly.

Billy's determination is admirable. But if he tries to do too much too soon, he is likely to slip backwards. (In fact, Billy won't be going back to the gym for several weeks.)

Every researcher on the subject of achievement and willpower speaks to the accomplishment of small, incremental goals on the way to a larger objective.

"Break the task into manageable chunks. A major contributor to (inaction) is a task that seems overwhelming. The solution is to divide the project into **small projects that seem less formidable.**

"You may have heard (of an) approach called the elephant technique. This technique is based on the … idea that eating an entire elephant in one sitting would be more than anyone could handle. A more sensible approach would be to eat the elephant one bite at a time."

Andrew DuBrin, PhD, *Getting It Done*
(Pacesetter Books, 1995)

"I don't love the elephant-for-dinner metaphor."

"I'm much more comfortable with Alan Lakein's swiss cheese metaphor."

"An excellent way to get moving is to turn (an over-whelming task) into 'swiss cheese' by poking some holes in it (little bites) … And once you've started, you've given yourself the opportunity to keep going. … Maybe all that was required was **to break up the task into manageable bites.…**

"If you must confront a difficult task, don't be concerned with conquering it (all at once). Be satisfied if you put up a better fight than you might have (in the past). **When you develop willpower, time is on your side if you improve just a little every day.**"

Alan Lakein, *How to Get Control of Your Time and Life* (Signet, 1973)

HERE IS THE MESSAGE:

THE PATH FROM WHERE YOU ARE TO WHERE YOU WANT TO BE IS MANY SMALL, MANAGEABLE STEPS. DON'T TRY TO RUN THE ENTIRE RACE IN ONE BURST. SLOW AND STEADY. THE KEY IS EASY-TO-DIGEST, INCREMENTAL BITES.

AS BILLY HAS PAINFULLY LEARNED, SOMETIMES YOU NEED SELF-DISCIPLINE TO KEEP YOUR IMPATIENCE IN CHECK AND MOVE FORWARD IN A REASONABLE FASHION.

115

THAT NIGHT

"Ow ... ow ... ow."   "Z z z z z"

116

"Let me tell you exactly what my website says about creating a willpower plan ...

and by the way, Beth, I'm only talky because I get really excited about trying to help!"

121

Although most people think of willpower as what you will need in the face of competing demands – and that is, of course, part of it – you can reduce both **the instances** when you need to utilize your will, and **the stress** involved when your will is tested, **by preparing yourself** for the challenge ahead.

Here is the preparation you need to do:

1. Identify **crisis points** and try to minimize them.

2. Create **preset mental responses** to crisis points.

3. Establish **a reinforcing mantra.**

4. Create **an anchor** – just in case you slip.

122

1. **Crisis Points** – These are those instances when you know that your willpower will be **especially tested**. In Billy's case, it is the presence of sweets. In Beth's case, she has trouble ignoring phone calls and emails when she is writing. So, she has learned to turn off her BlackBerry when she is working on her business plan.

2. **Preset responses** – Plan **exactly how you will react** when a crisis point arises. If Billy creates a willpower plan, he should prepare for instances when he is out to dinner and others are having dessert; e.g., he might have a rule to always ask for fruit every time he is with others having dessert.

3. **Reinforcing mantra** – This is a **word or phrase to use** when you are at a crisis point, you have tried your preset response technique and you still feel your willpower waning. For example, when Beth forgets to turn off her BlackBerry and she gets a call from a friend, she is really tempted to stop writing and talk. So she remembers her mantra, "Beth's Boutique," says it over and over, and ignores the phone.

4. **Anchor** – There may well be times when all else fails and we give in to temptations. But **that does not mean "game over"**. The sooner we get back on course, the better. Since it is possible that you will slip, prepare a speech to yourself in advance: "OK, Billy, you messed up ... no big deal ... now just jump right back into your diet and exercise program."

The point is that by creating preset responses to use when you are stressed, you **reduce the amount of will-power** you need to succeed in the achievement of your goal!

"Well, I must admit that a willpower plan does make sense ... I just don't want that Randel guy dropping in on us again."

"Whoops ... time for a U-turn."

That evening

"Beth, you seem to be making good progress on your business plan."

"Yes, I'm actually almost finished."

"Well, I also went on Randel's website, and I learned about something called 'ego depletion.'"

???

132

"You see, willpower is like a muscle that can get fatigued. So, it's usually not a good idea to take on too many challenges at once."

133

"Hey, Billy, I'm happy that you visited my website. And you are right about Beth – it's probably not a great idea for her to start on a diet while she is using so much willpower writing her business plan.

"Let me tell you a bit more of the history and thinking on willpower being just like a muscle."

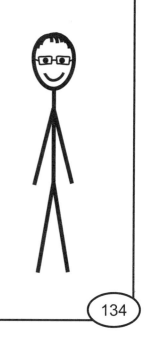

134

The idea that willpower is muscle-like was first proposed by psychologists about 30 years ago.

Test subjects were put into situations in which they needed self-discipline, and then immediately thereafter placed in new situations requiring additional self-discipline. What psychologists found was that in a succession of challenges, one's willpower is depleted ("ego depletion"). In other words, like a muscle, willpower use was fatiguing.

I'd like to tell you about one famous study you may find interesting.

135

One hundred people were randomly divided into three groups.

Each member of Group A was given a plate of radishes and asked to eat all of them.

Each member of Group B was given a plate of cookies and asked to eat all of them.

Each member of Group C was given the choice of eating whatever he or she wanted, or nothing.

After all the radishes and cookies were consumed, everyone was given the same brainteaser to solve (which actually had no solution).

While the people in Groups B and C were able to work at the brainteaser for about 15 minutes before giving up, the people in Group A threw in the towel after only seven minutes.

The researchers concluded from this experiment that the members of Group A had depleted their willpower eating all the (bitter) radishes, while the members of Groups B and C still had lots of willpower left to struggle with the brainteaser.

The lesson is to preserve your willpower for those situations where you need it most.

"The question I asked myself as I was reading all the literature on willpower and 'ego depletion' was whether willpower – if it is really like a muscle – could be built up in strength like any other muscle.

"So I called a well-known authority on the subject of willpower and self-discipline (psychologists use the term 'self-regulation'), Dr. Roy Baumeister of Florida State University."

"Tell me, Doctor, is there evidence that people can build up their willpower like a muscle?"

"Well, some psychologists have done research indicating that exercises in self-control, such as performing simple tasks with one's nondominant hand, can gradually improve one's willpower for other tasks."

Dr. Roy Baumeister

I pressed Dr. Baumeister on this subject: I asked whether he recommended that people do willpower-building exercises.

He responded that more study was needed before he could give a conclusive answer to my question.

He did feel strongly, however, that good health and self-control were connected, and he referred me to a book he had edited, *The Handbook of Self-Regulation: Research, Theory and Applications* (Guilford Press, 2004).

Here is an excerpt:

"Other work is needed to explore how the self-regulatory resource may be replenished when it is temporarily depleted. Although systematic studies are lacking, circumstantial evidence indicates that sleep and other forms of rest help restore it…. One study found that guided meditation helped to offset the impact of ego depletion and to restore (one's reserve of self-regulation)."

Roy Baumeister and Brandon Schmeichel

Although Doctor Baumeister is unsure of the connection between willpower-building exercises and the availability of willpower when you need it, others feel differently.

For example, Ramez Sasson is a writer whose e-Book, *Willpower and Self-Discipline* (2008), lists 80 exercises one can do to build willpower.

Here is what Sasson believes: "The methods of this book can be compared to physical training."

Sasson maintains that anyone who works at the described exercises will build self-discipline for important challenges.

Here are a few of Sasson's suggested exercises:

#1 Itching and Scratching

The desire to scratch can be real strong and disturbing. Postpone the scratching for as long as you can.

"My nose REALLY itches!!!"

#2 Driving behind a slow vehicle

Drive slowly and patiently behind the slow car. It might not be easy, especially when you are in a hurry.

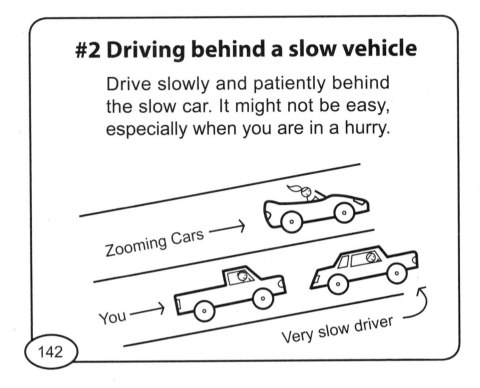

Zooming Cars

You

Very slow driver

#3 Using your nondominant hand

You are temporarily acting contrary to a habit in order to gain inner strength.

"Hey, Billy, your ping-pong game is really off today."

Everyone should decide for himself or herself how they feel about willpower-building exercises.

To some, the idea of building willpower by increasing one's capacity for frustration (e.g., playing ping-pong with your nondominant hand) makes a lot of sense. In fact, although willpower as a muscle has only been studied for about 30 years, here is an excerpt from a book written **110 years ago**:

"Self-control may be developed by precisely the same manner as we tone a weak muscle, by little exercises day by day. Let us do each day … a few acts that are disagreeable to us, the doing of which will help us in our hour of need."

The Kingship of Self-Control, William George Jordan (1899).

Me, I always worry about preservation of energy. I work under the premise that we all have a finite capacity for frustration. Accordingly, I personally try to minimize frustration in my life (the little things), so that I will have plenty of resolve for the big stuff. For example, when I play ping-pong, I use my right hand.

"Hey Randel, nice shot!"

Some people go much too far in trying to build willpower muscles.

G. Gordon Liddy was a CIA operative who is best known for his role in the 1968 Watergate affair, which toppled President Richard Nixon.

Liddy believed that by holding his hand over an open flame – for progressively longer periods – he could build his resolve for anything.

"I had begun by using ... matches and candles, progressively increasing the time I exposed my body to pain as I built up my will, much as one might build muscles by lifting increasingly heavy weights."

Will: The Autobiography of G. Gordon Liddy,
G. Gordon Liddy (Macmillan, 1991)

Liddy actually did permanent damage to his hands.

"That kind of behavior is nuts ... do not do anything like that!"

A few days later

"Beth, you must be almost finished with your business plan by now!"

Happily, Billy said just the right thing.

We all have fears of varying types and degrees. But we can defeat these fears.

The point is to develop the strength of mind – the mental fortitude – to conquer fear.

I have identified five steps for building mental fortitude.

1. Awareness

At critical times, when you feel yourself pulled in a direction you know not to be in your best interest, take a deep breath and look inside yourself. What are the exact thoughts that are affecting your behavior? Where do they come from?

Identify **exactly those thoughts** that are controlling your conduct.

2. Recognize that thoughts are things

One of the most successful self-help books of the last 100 years is titled *Think & Grow Rich*, written in 1937 by Napoleon Hill. This book (which is only partly about making money) has sold more than 60 million copies.

The key point of this book is that you control your destiny when you **learn to control your mind**.

And the way to control your mind is by understanding that **thoughts are things, just like any other physical object**, and therefore, they can be moved in and out of your mind as you see fit.

3. Understand that there is clutter in all of our minds

The mind is **a receptacle of all sorts of thoughts**, some good … some junk.

The junky thoughts are those that hold you back.

There are also other thoughts – dreams of the person you want to be. These are the thoughts you want to cultivate.

4. Acknowledge that you are running the show

As you listen to your thoughts, you begin to realize that **you are not your thoughts**. Rather, you are the higher form listening to your thoughts – and therefore, you can separate yourself from them.

As Eckhart Tolle says in *The Power of Now* (Namaste, 1999): "When you listen to a thought, you are aware of yourself as a witness to the thought. The thought then loses its power over you."

In other words, you, as the force listening to the thoughts, have control over them. You can decide which ones you want to accept, and which ones you want to reject.

5. Know that your mind can only process one dominant thought at a time

By controlling those thoughts that dominate your thinking, you can have an enormous impact on your conduct.

By **subjugating negative thoughts to one powerful and positive dominant thought**, you push the right message to the forefront of your consciousness.

For example, if fear of taking action is a problem (as it is for Beth), a mechanism for defeating that fear is to overwhelm it with one strong dominating thought, such as the image of you successfully completing a challenge.

I recognize that mind control and mental fortitude are big subjects. I am giving you the key points now but there is a bibliography in the back of the book with suggestions for further reading.

The point is that **you have the ability to take owner-ship of the free flow of thoughts in your mind, what I call "the noise." You can pick and choose those thoughts you want to be conscious of, and those that you don't.**

Fears that are holding you back – OUT.

Confidence and optimism about a successful conclusion to your challenge – IN.

"Do you think that a few examples would be helpful?"

"Yes!"

"OK, then. Let's talk a bit more about mind control, which some would say is the root of all willpower."

"Well, what's interesting is the subtitle:

*Why You Lose Your Car Keys ...
and Other Puzzles of Everyday Life.*"

"No."

"No."

173

"This book teaches us about dominating thoughts ... Because Beth is so focused on her business plan, she has no room in her mind to think about where she puts her car keys."

174

They do that by following the five steps I have identified.

1. They are **aware** of what is going on in their mind at critical times.

2. They **recognize that thoughts are things** – things that can be moved around.

3. They know that **at times, negativism clutters the mind**.

4. They have learned that **the person hearing the noise is in charge**.

5. They are trained to **insert dominating positive thoughts when challenged**.

"Billy likes football, so let's talk about place-kickers. They have to perform under enormous pressure in short bursts when lots of fans are screaming at them."

181

"But they exercise dominion over harmful thoughts and kick them out of their mind (good pun, huh?), replacing any negativity with a positive dominating thought."

182

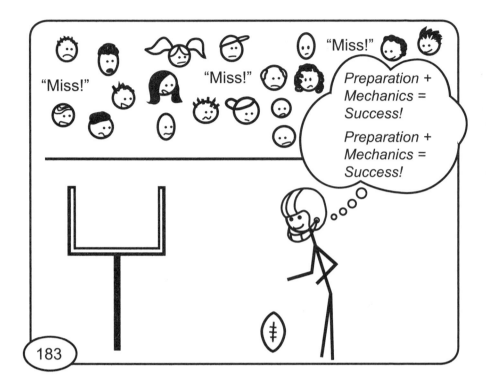

"One key to achieving success in sports is learning how to focus on the task and not let negative thoughts intrude. **The mind can concentrate on only one thing at a time** ... You must focus on what you do want to happen or on some neutral thought. In working with placekickers, I use a distraction technique.

"I ask them to create a word that, when said to themselves, **will block out all negative thoughts** ..."

Mind Gym, Gary Mack and David Casstevens
(McGraw-Hill, 2001)

"But, Jimbo, those guys are professionals. They are trained in mind control ... "

"Billy, they are no different than you and I. They are experts in a specific physical activity. Mind control can be learned by anyone."

187

"Let me give you one more example of how an ordinary man used mind control and fortitude to save his sanity ... and his life."

188

Victor Frankl was a German psychiatrist who was sent to a concentration camp during World War II because he was Jewish.

For three years Frankl struggled to survive, and in 1946 after the War, he wrote a very powerful book about his experience, titled *Man's Search for Meaning*.

In this book, Frankl speaks to mind control – about how he was able to move his thoughts from the horror of his imprisonment to another place and time. Whereas the noise was still there in his mind – the feelings and emotions of his existence – his consciousness was elevated to a place and time far away.

189

"I kept thinking of the endless little problems of our miserable life ... If a piece of sausage came as an extra ration, should I exchange it for a piece of bread? Should I trade my last cigarette for a bowl of soup? How could I get a piece of wire (for a shoelace)?

"I became disgusted with the state of affairs which compelled me, daily and hourly, to think of only such trivial things. **I forced my thoughts to turn to another subject**. Suddenly, I saw myself standing on the plat-form of a well-lit, warm and pleasant lecture room.... By this method, I succeeded somehow **in rising above the situation**, above the sufferings of the moment."

Victor Frankl (Emphasis Added)

190

"Willpower is directly connected to mind control.

"Once you realize that you have the ability to eject negative thoughts from your mind and inject positive thoughts into the void, you have taken a gigantic step toward a lifetime of self-discipline as and when you need it."

"I'll see you guys later."

Billy at the gym

Like many people, Sammy is looking for some kind of a shortcut – an easy path from where he is to where he wants to be.

But, almost by definition, there are no shortcuts. The fact is that those accomplishments which are the hardest to achieve are the most desired.

As the American Revolutionary Thomas Paine (author of the hugely popular pamphlet, *Common Sense*) said:

"That which we obtain too easily, we esteem too lightly. It is dearness only which gives everything its value. Heaven knows how to put a proper price on its goods."

Thomas Paine

The people who accomplish the most, who achieve their goals and dreams, are those who have the self-discipline and willpower to take the right actions and make the right choices, **especially when it is difficult to do so**.

In almost all cases, achievement is just a story of hard work, persistence and willpower.

Beth at the Bank

"I'm impressed, Mrs. Branch. I think we can make this loan. We will, of course, need liens on your house, your car, your jewelry, and your husband's baseball card collection."

Two months later

Unfortunately, not "The End"

I'd like to tell you that Billy and Beth lived happily ever after and never had challenges again. But, hey, this isn't a comic book.

Unfortunately, Billy had troubles with his boss at work, and as a result, he started overeating. And Beth's business struggled when the economy softened a few months after she opened.

You see life is really a succession of challenges. The goal is to deal with these challenges in a positive way and keep moving forward.

Fortunately, what Billy and Beth had learned about willpower was very helpful to them.

Billy eventually got back on his diet, and Beth worked her way through her financial troubles!

Now ...

"The End"

Good news!

After Beth got through her financial troubles, her business began to prosper, and she and Billy decided to start a family!

"Before we say 'good-bye,' I would like to summarize for you what I have learned after many years of studying the subject of willpower.

"What follows is my 15-Point Plan for improving your willpower and self-discipline.

"I present these points to you as my ideas to help you develop the resolve you need for whatever challenge you choose to undertake."

"Best of Luck!"

1

Be sure you are totally committed.

People who truly "set their mind" activate certain energies that give them strength for achievement.

Many who think they make a sincere commitment to their goal really don't. For example, some people who say "I am on a diet," really mean "I will avoid fattening foods when it is convenient for me to do so." **That is not a commitment.**

Napoleon Hill (*Think & Grow Rich*) suggested that one needs "white-hot desire" to be successful.

The amount of willpower you will have when you want it is a function of how committed you are to your goal and the value you place on that goal. Remember what Professor Reeve taught us – if we have a high degree of internal motivation (we are driven by values we hold dearly), we are very likely to have the willpower we need.

But, if you are not 100% committed to the achievement of a goal, why bother starting? Wait for another time when you are really, really ready!

2

Prepare yourself for a difficult journey.

Those who expect positive results too quickly or easily often falter. If, on the other hand, you expect the road to be "long and winding," you are not easily blown off course.

"It hurts my heart when I think about people who have had incredible ideas, but give up because things don't pop off right away. Try to remember that nothing worthwhile is ever going to just pop off."

Do You! Russell Simmons (Gotham, 2007)

I believe that the great succeeders in life are those who, as Scott Peck identified, understand that "life is difficult" and make a lifelong commitment to fight the hurdles and adversities they confront.

As written by William James:

"(Some people) choose their attitude and **know that the facing of its difficulties shall remain a permanent portion of their task** … They find a zest in this difficult clinging to truth, or a lonely sort of joy in pressing on the thorn ... And thereby they become the masters and the lords of life. They must be counted with henceforth; they form a part of human destiny."

3

Prepare for your challenge by reducing the instances in which you will need to exert willpower.

Willpower is all about energy, and if you limit the number of times you have to actually expend willpower, you preserve your strength for when you really need it.

Here are some ideas for preserving energy:

(1) Create some black-and-white rules – in other words, do what you can to reduce deliberation in stressful circumstances.

(2) Establish rituals – prepare for certain situations by setting in advance how you will respond. "If X happens, I will do Y."

(3) Develop a mantra – a word or phrase to repeat to yourself when you feel yourself weakening.

(4) Strategize an anchor – build an immediate path back to your journey if you should stray off course.

If I were to identify one technique that has helped me find resolve when I need it, it is a **trigger or pre-set response** to the first sensation of a negative impulse (like laziness). The instant I feel it, I push back. With time, this reflex has helped me stay on track by keeping harmful pressures or cravings in check.

4

Identify your goal and the process to get there in as concrete, specific and finite terms as possible.

The mind works best when it **knows exactly what it needs to do**.

Numerous studies have established that those who have a concrete and specific goal are more likely to reach that goal.

In addition, the mind is most comfortable when it can see the end of its journey. Be clear with yourself as to what constitutes success and how long it may take.

In a painfully powerful illustration of this point, Victor Frankl, in his book about survival in a concentration camp, related that the one week in camp when the most prisoners died was the last week of the year. That was because many prisoners had convinced themselves that they would be home by year-end, and when it became clear that was not going to happen, the inmates just gave up.

In other words, when the end line was finite, the prisoners found the strength to keep going. But, when the end line moved (and the goal was no longer a specific distance away), their will to live evaporated.

5

Divide your challenge into small, manageable pieces.

The way to achieve a large goal is to break it into parts – each segment being a challenge, athough not too far beyond your present capabilities.

By way of example, if you have never run a race before and your goal is to run a marathon, you should train first to run one mile, then five and so on. If you try to run too far too early in your training, you may become discouraged and never achieve your goal.

This example is a metaphor for any challenge.

When starting off in pursuit of a goal, **identify logical break points along the way**. As you achieve each sub-goal, stop and breathe the air of success. This will give you the confidence for the next stage of your journey.

"In your journey to personal excellence, it is best to focus most of your energy on taking little steps that are within your control – to improve your skills, your preparation, your execution, your routines – and to be the best you can be that day."

In Pursuit of Excellence,
Terry Orlick (Human
Kinetics, 2000)

You were going to eat me??

6

Maintain vigilance over your thoughts.

There is a lot of noise in our minds, some of which can weaken our resolve.

By keeping aware of what is going on in your mind when you feel yourself faltering, you minimize the risk that you will actually give up.

"Once goal-setting has been developed, the ability to self-monitor becomes essential because attention to internal and external cues through greater self-awareness leads to faster and more appropriate control ... **The basis of self-regulation (the element attempting to guide behavior along a specific path to a directed aim or goal) is self-monitoring.**"

Self-Regulation, Luke Behnke, RMIT University, (Melbourne, Australia, 2002) (Emphasis Added)

Learning to control your mind is one of the most important elements for success in any endeavor. As Tiger Woods said in his book *How I Play Golf* (Sphere, 2001): "Mental toughness ... gift to my game from my dad. He wanted to make sure that my powers of concentration could withstand any and all distractions."

7

Control your dominant thoughts.

You need to **think about thoughts as things** because once you do, it is easier to conceptualize physically evicting from your mind negative thoughts and replacing them with positive imagery.

As Dr. Terry Orlick writes in his book on performance excellence, "We can learn to shift focus … If you practice this often in a variety of settings, you will definitely increase your effectiveness."

Or, as Napoleon Hill said: "Mind control is the result of self-discipline and habit. You either control your mind or it controls you. There is no halfway compromise. The most practical of all methods for controlling the mind is the habit of keeping it busy with a definite purpose…."

And here is one of my favorite quotes from a book titled
Strength in the Storm by Eknath Easwaren:

"The faculty of voluntarily bringing back a wandering attention, over and over again, is the very root of judgment, character, and will. … (this) is the secret of life: the key to genius, to success, to love, to happiness, to security, to fulfillment. We live where our attention is … complete concentration is the secret of genius in any field. **Those who can put their attention on a task or goal and keep it there are bound to make their mark in life**." (Emphasis Added)

Frame your challenges in a pleasurable, not painful, manner.

How we communicate with ourselves is critical. Some of those who speak or write about willpower propose Neuro-Linguistic Programming (NLP) as a way to **frame challenges so that they are easier to overcome.**

If you see the path to the goal ahead of you as boring and painful, you will most certainly fail. On the other hand, if you can frame the journey as an enjoyable experience, you are much more likely to stay the course.

The most famous proponent of NLP is Tony Robbins, perhaps best known for teaching people to walk on hot coals.

"The key to producing the results you desire ... is to represent things to yourself in a way that puts you in such a resourceful state that you're empowered to take the types and qualities of actions that create your desired outcomes."

Unlimited Power, Tony Robbins (Fireside, 1986)

9

Pick your spots.

There will be times in your life when your willpower tank will be low.

Research (remember the radish study) has established that upon exerting a lot of willpower, one needs to recover before taking on a new task that requires self-discipline.

So, **be selective** in how you use willpower in the short term. If you are engaged in or have just finished a difficult challenge, don't take on anything new that will require a lot of resolve.

Give yourself time to recover and build your strength back. If, for example, you have just finished studying for and taking a college exam, wait a while before you start an exercise program.

"One interesting aspect of the finiteness of willpower is that a variety of tasks call upon the same reserves … effortful willpower of any kind interferes with effortful willpower of any other kind immediately thereafter …"

Welcome to Your Brain, Aamodt and Wang (Bloomsbury, 2008)

10

Force yourself to visualize the end of a succession of "either/or" choices.

Increase your willpower when you are challenged by forcing yourself to **visualize the end of the story** that results from each of the choices you are confronted with.

In every situation, you can either do A or B. You can eat the dessert or not. You can sleep late or not. You can start your homework or not. You can quit your exercise program or not. And so on, with infinite possibilities.

The way I stay on point when I feel my resolve weaken is to force myself to visualize different versions of me after a succession of right or wrong choices. A fit me or a sloppy me. A financially comfortable me or a struggling me. A relaxed me or a tense me.

As soon as I feel lazy or tempted by a negative choice, I press into my mind two pictures – the one I want to live, and the one I don't.

Willpower is about making the right choices at the right times.

11

You already have more willpower than you realize.

There are innumerable stories of people who accomplished incredible acts of willpower because "they had to."

Never say to yourself:

"I don't have the willpower or self-discipline to do that."

The fact is that **you do have it**; it is simply in reserve, waiting for the time when you fully engage with a goal that is extremely important to you.

Here is a great quote from William James:

"We are making use of only a small part of our physical and mental resources … (we all live) far within our limits. We all have reservoirs of energy and genius to draw upon of which we do not dream."

Or, as stated by William George Jordan:

"Reserve power is a gradual and constant revelation of strength within us to meet each new need."

The more you use your willpower, the more confidence and strength you have for new challenges.

Some psychologists analogize willpower to a muscle. The more we use it, to the point of fatigue, the stronger it becomes.

Personally, I do not believe in performing willpower exercises *just for the sake of* building up your ability to resist temptation and frustration.

However, I do believe that the process of challenging yourself – in incrementally more difficult tests – will **expand your capacity for new achievement**. That is because each time you accomplish something challenging, you gain confidence and strength for a more difficult test. Eventually your resolve and self-discipline are ready for just about anything life chooses to throw at you.

"Willpower isn't something that gets handed out to some and not to others… it's a skill you can develop through understanding and practice. … Facing any willpower challenge opens up endless possibilities ... you develop greater trust and a more positive regard for yourself."

Gillian Riley

— 13 —

Turn positive activity into habits.

Remember how inertia can work in your favor. **As you build repetition into your life, through regular conduct, habits will develop**.

The great thing about habits is that once they become ingrained, they do not require much willpower.

What was once a chore – e.g., exercise on a constant basis – becomes as much a part of your life as brushing your teeth. When that happens you can put your strength and focus toward new challenges.

"We are what we repeatedly do. Excellence, then, is not an act, but a habit."

Aristotle

14

Self-discipline is not self-deprivation.

Some people think of self-discipline as the constant refusal of life's pleasures.

I don't think of it that way. To me, self-discipline is not about gratification denied ... it is about gratification delayed.

Self-discipline is about doing things **today** that may not be your "first choice," for the pleasure of experiencing bigger and better things **tomorrow**.

Of course, each of us needs to find a balance between immediate and deferred gratification ... in other words, we do the best we can.

"Some people feel that discipline is a dirty word, but it shouldn't be. All it really means is doing what you are supposed to do in the best possible manner at the time you are supposed to do it. And that's not a bad thing."

Mike Krzyzewski, Coach of the Duke basketball team, *Leading with the Heart* (Warner Books, 2000)

— 15 —

Strong willpower can take you to new heights in life.

A strong self-discipline can take you places you never knew you were capable of going. Those who develop willpower and self-discipline **expand their horizons**. The breadth of what they can accomplish is widened, opening doors for great material and spiritual achievement.

With challenge and achievement comes personal fulfillment and happiness:

"Capacities clamor to be used, and cease their clamor only when they are."

Toward a Psychology of Being, Abraham Maslow (Wiley, 1999)

"Our inborn potential as humans dictates that we do more, that we utilize our full capacities."

Happier: Learn the Secrets to Daily Joy and Lasting Fulfillment, Tal Ben-Shahar, (McGraw-Hill, 2007)

"The best moments usually occur when a person's body or mind is stretched to its limits in a voluntary effort to accomplish something difficult and worthwhile."

Flow, Mihaly Csikszentmihalyi (Rider, 1992)

CONCLUSION

You really don't have a choice.

If you want to survive, let alone prosper, in the 21st century, you need to be the best you can be. And that means developing your willpower and self-discipline so you can deal with whatever opportunities or setbacks life throws at you.

Willpower is nothing more than the ability to take appropriate action in the face of competing pressures. And the good news is that whatever the challenge or opportunity ahead of you, you can build your willpower to achieve what you set out for.

We hope that our "skinny" book has been helpful in giving you ideas for building your own willpower.

Please visit our website for further information. Also, please feel free to e-mail me at jrandel@theskinnyon.com.

I would love to hear from you.

With all best wishes,

Jim Randel

AUTHOR BIO

Jim Randel, 60, is a graduate of Columbia Law School.

He has made his living as an entrepreneur – buying and selling commercial real estate and starting new businesses.

Addressing the subjects of investing and entrepreneurism, Randel has been a speaker at many venues around the United States, including Harvard and NYU Business Schools.

Randel is a 30-year student of the subject of achievement. In addition to reading all that he can find on the subject, he pesters successful people with questions about their own path to success (until they excuse themselves). The conclusions in this book are the result of years of study, personal experimentation and learning from others.

Randel has concluded that the secret to achievement is one of desire, hard work, grit, determination and persistence … all of which require willpower and self-discipline.

Randel believes that all things are possible if one is willing to pay the price.

BIBLIOGRAPHY

Here are some of the resources that went into the research for *The Skinny on Willpower*:

A Guide to Rational Living, Ellis and Harper (Wilshire Book Company, 1961)

A New Earth: Awakening to Your Life's Purpose, Eckhart Tolle (Plume, 2005)

Bird by Bird, Anne Lamott (Anchor Books, 1995)

Discipline: Six Steps to Unleashing Your Hidden Potential, Harris Kern (1st Books, 2001)

Discipline: Training the Mind to Manage Your Life, Kern and Willi (1st Books, 2002)

Do You! 12 Laws to Access the Power in You to Achieve Happiness and Success, Russell Simmons (Gotham, 2008)

Emotional Intelligence, Daniel Goleman (Bantam Books, 1994)

Flow: The Psychology of Optimal Experience, Mihaly Csikszentmihalyi (Harper Perennial, 1991)

Getting It Done: The Transforming Power of Self-Discipline, Andrew DuBrin (Peterson's Guides, 1997)

Happier: Learn the Secrets to Daily Joy and Lasting Fulfillment, Tal Ben-Shahar (McGraw-Hill, 2007)

How to Get Control of Your Time and Life, Alan Lakein (Signet, 1973)

In Pursuit of Excellence, Terry Orlick (Human Kinetics, 2000)

Leading With the Heart, Mike Krzyzewski (Warner Books, 2000)

Man's Search for Meaning, Victor Frankl (Simon & Schuster, 1946)

Mind Gym : An Athlete's Guide to Inner Excellence, Gary Mack and David Casstevens (McGraw-Hill, 2001)

Mindset: The New Psychology of Success, Carol Dweck (Ballantine, 2006)

On Writing, Stephen King (Pocket Books, 2000)

Seeds of Greatness, Denis Waitley (Pocket Books, 1983)

Self-Discipline in 10 Days: How to Go from Thinking to Doing, Theodore Bryant (HUB Publishing, 2004)

Self-Reliance, Ralph Waldo Emerson (1842)

Spark: The Revolutionary New Science of Exercise and the Brain, John Ratey (Little, Brown & Company, 2008)

Success: Advice for Achieving your Goals from Remarkably Successful People, Jena Pincott (Random House, 2005)

Success is a Choice, Rick Pitino (Broadway, 1997)

The Black Swan, Nassim Taleb (Random House, 2007)

The Brain that Changes Itself, Norman Doidge (Penguin, 2007)

The Creative Habit, Twyla Tharp (Simon & Schuster, 2003)

The Dip: A Little Book that Teaches You When to Quit (And When to Stick), Seth Godin (Penguin, 2007)

The Magic of Thinking Big, Daniel Schwartz (Simon & Schuster, 1959)

The New Toughness Training for Sports, James Loehr (Plume, 1995)

The Power of Full Engagement: Managing Energy, Not Time, Is the Key to High Performance and Personal Renewal, Loehr and Schwartz (Free Press, 2003)

The Power of Intention, Wayne Dyer (Hay House, 2004)

The Power of Now: A Guide to Spiritual Enlightenment, Eckhart Tolle (Namaste, 1999)

The Power of Positive Thinking, Norman Vincent Peale (Fawcett, 1952)

The Practicing Mind: Bringing Discipline and Focus Into Your Life, Thomas Sterner (Mountain Sage, 2005)

The Science of Self-Discipline (CD), Kerry Johnson (Nightingale Conant, 1995)

The Seven Habits of Highly Effective People, Stephen Covey (Simon & Schuster, 1989)

The Success Principles, Jack Canfield (HarperCollins, 2005)

The TOPS Way to Weight Loss, Howard Rankin (Hay House, 2004)

The Way to Wealth, Brian Tracy (Entrepreneur Press, 2007)

Think and Grow Rich, Napoleon Hill (Fawcett, 1937)

Tiger Woods: How I Play Golf (Sphere, 2001)

Toward a Psychology of Being, Abraham Maslow (Wiley, 1968)

True Success: A New Philosophy of Excellence, Tom Morris (Berkley, 1994)

Understanding Motivation and Emotion, Johnmarshall Reeve (Wiley, 2008)

Unleash the Warrior Within: Develop the Focus, Discipline, Confidence, and Courage You Need to Achieve Unlimited Goals, Richard Machowicz (Perseus, 2000)

Unlimited Power: The New Science Of Personal Achievement, Tony Robbins (Fireside, 1986)

Welcome to Your Brain, Aamodt and Wang (Bloomsbury, 2008)

Will: The Autobiography of G. Gordon Liddy, G. Gordon Liddy (Macmillan, 1991)

William James: In the Maelstrom of American Modernism, Robert Richardson (Houghton Mifflin, 2007)

Willpower, Gillian Riley (Vermillion, 2003)

Willpower and Self-Discipline, Remez Sasson (successconsciousness.com, 2007)

Willpower is Not Enough, A. Dean Byrd and Mark D. Chamberlain (Deseret, 1995)

Your Erroneous Zones, Wayne Dyer (Avon, 1995)

Zen, Chris Prentiss (Power Press, 2006)